AMAZING SCIENCE
OCEANS

Written by Alex Hall

Genius Kid

American adaptation copyright © 2026 by North Star Editions, Mendota Heights, MN 55120. All rights reserved. No part of this book may be reproduced or utilized in any form or by any means without written permission from the publisher.

Oceans © 2024 BookLife Publishing
This edition is published by arrangement with BookLife Publishing

sales@northstareditions.com | 888-417-0195

Library of Congress Control Number:
2024952961

ISBN
978-1-952455-26-1 (library bound)
978-1-952455-82-7 (paperback)
978-1-952455-64-3 (epub)
978-1-952455-46-9 (hosted ebook)

Printed in the United States of America
Mankato, MN
092025

Written by:
Alex Hall

Edited by:
Elise Carraway

Designed by:
Ker Ker Lee

All facts, statistics, web addresses and URLs in this book were verified as valid and accurate at time of writing. No responsibility for any changes to external websites or references can be accepted by either the author or publisher.

Photo Credits – Images courtesy of Shutterstock.com, unless otherwise stated.

Cover – Seashell World, Aleksandr Simonov, Eric Isselee, RHJPhtotos, ARoxoPT, Rich Carey, Animalgraphy, Mr.wutthiphat vimuktanont, LedyX, Nazarii_Neshcherenskyi, BJP7images, Ekky Ilhamw, Tatiana Gnuchykh. 2–3 – Irina Markova, Zhane Luk. 4–5 – Peter Hermes Furian, Photoongraphy, karacacennet. 6–7 – tomtomdotcom_tbirdaerial, Indi_kator, Delbars, Bing Wen, Vintagepix. 8–9 – Gulf MG, Hamizan Yusof, Zhane Luk, Lea McQuillan. 10–11 – lunamarina, Martin Prochazkacz, Delz76, Planicauda, Miroslav Halama, Dmitry Rukhlenko. 12–13 – Tomas Ragina, Neil Bromhall. 14–15 – RHJPhtotos, EVGEIIA, Ethan Daniels. 16–17 – Julian Gunther, SpicyTruffel, Surkhab Ahmad Art. 18–19 – Olga Kuevda, Ivan Marc, Leo Wehrli, CC BY-SA 4.0 <https://creativecommons.org/licenses/by-sa/4.0>, via Wikimedia Commons, Berann, Heinrich C., Heezen, Bruce C., Tharp, Marie., CC0, via Wikimedia Commons. 20–21 – DrShutter, Ekky Ilham, Rebecca Schreiner. 22–23 – STUDIO DREAM, Khosro, MyBestCollection, Benny Marty, maya_parf, LeonP.

CONTENTS

Page 4   Oceans
Page 6   Key Words
Page 8   Sunlight Zone
Page 10   Twilight Zone
Page 12   Midnight Zone
Page 14   Abyssal Zone
Page 16   Hadal Zone
Page 18   A Timeline of Ocean Exploration
Page 20   Believe It or Not!
Page 22   Are You a Genius Kid?
Page 24   Glossary and Index

Words that look like <u>this</u> can be found in the glossary on page 24.

OCEANS

Close your eyes and picture Earth. What colors do you see?

Earth is mostly covered with blue oceans. It is even nicknamed the blue planet! But what is an ocean?

An ocean is a large body of salt water.

Earth has five oceans, but they are all connected. Our oceans are called:

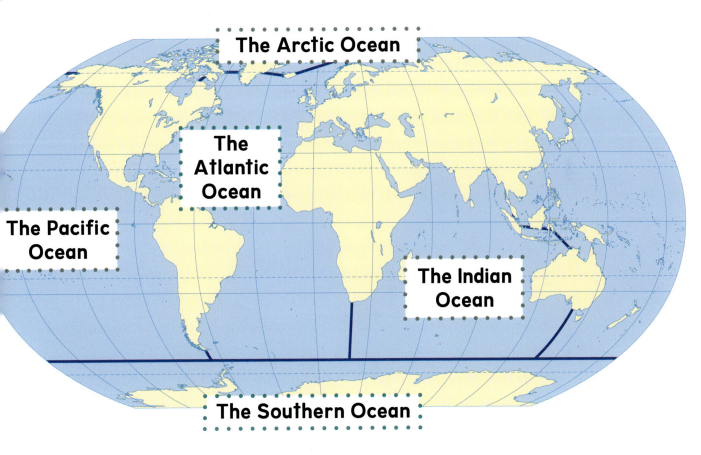

The Pacific Ocean is the largest ocean.

DID YOU KNOW?
Most of Earth's water is found in oceans.

5

KEY WORDS

Here are some key words about oceans that every genius kid should learn.

COAST
The coast is the area of land next to the sea.

CURRENTS
Oceans are always moving. The direction the water moves is called the current.

TIDE

The tide is the way the ocean rises and falls throughout the day.

At high tide, the water covers a lot of the beach.

At low tide, the sea is far out.

WAVES

The wind can make the ocean move.
Movements on top of the water are called waves.

SUNLIGHT ZONE

Oceans are split into different layers. The layer nearest to the <u>surface</u> is called the sunlight zone. It is the warmest layer of the ocean.

The sunlight zone is from the top of the ocean to around 660 feet down.

The sunlight zone is a small part of the ocean. It is home to many living things. These include turtles, seagrass, and seaweed.

Coral reefs are found in the sunlight zone. Coral reefs are warm underwater habitats. They are made of living things called coral polyps.

TWILIGHT ZONE

The layer below the sunlight zone is the twilight zone. This zone is from about 660 to 3,300 feet deep.

The twilight zone does not get much sunlight. Hardly any plants grow at this layer.

Large animals live in the twilight zone. Sperm whales and giant squid call this layer home.

Many animals that live in this layer have large eyes that point upward. This helps them see creatures moving around above them.

Some animals at this layer can make their own light. This is called bioluminescence.

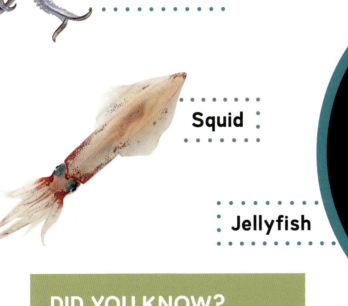

Cuttlefish

Squid

Jellyfish

DID YOU KNOW?
Some twilight zone animals <u>migrate</u> to the surface at night.

MIDNIGHT ZONE

Below the twilight zone is the midnight zone. This layer is from 3,300 to 13,100 feet deep.

The midnight zone is the largest ocean layer. It contains almost three-fourths of the world's water.

The midnight zone is always 39 degrees Fahrenheit.

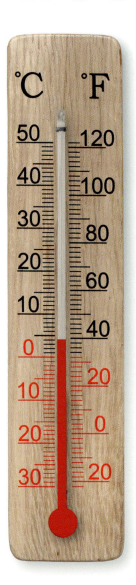

It is difficult to explore deep layers of the ocean. Scientists use remote-controlled vehicles to explore the midnight zone.

Some animals in the midnight zone have lures. Lures are bioluminescent body parts that attract fish to eat.

ABYSSAL ZONE

The abyssal zone goes from 13,100 to 19,700 feet deep. It often goes down to the seafloor. The seafloor is not flat. There are dips in the ground called trenches. They can go very deep.

DID YOU KNOW?
The seafloor has some mountains and <u>volcanoes</u>.

The seafloor is full of useful <u>minerals</u>, such as aluminum and nickel. It might be possible to collect them in the future.

aluminum

DID YOU KNOW?
The name *abyssal* comes from a Greek word. It means "no bottom." People used to think the ocean was bottomless.

nickel

HADAL ZONE

The hadal zone is the lowest layer. It's more than 19,700 feet deep. Only some trenches go down that far.

There are no plants in the hadal zone. But some animals live there.

DID YOU KNOW?
The hadal zone is named after a Greek god called Hades.

The deepest known point in the ocean is the bottom of the Mariana Trench. This trench is in the Pacific Ocean. It reaches a depth of almost 36,070 feet.

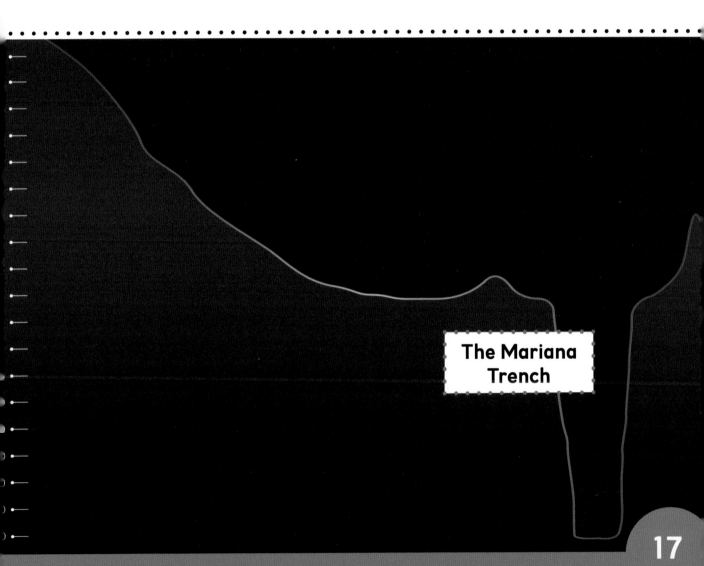

The Mariana Trench

A TIMELINE OF OCEAN EXPLORATION

Around 4000 BCE
Ancient Egyptians made some of the first sailing boats.

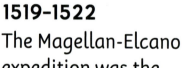

1519–1522
The Magellan-Elcano <u>expedition</u> was the first trip that sailed all the way around Earth.

Around 1000 CE
The Vikings sailed to North America.

1620
Cornelis Drebbel made the first submarine. It could go 13 feet underwater.

1930s
William Beebe set a record by diving 3,028 feet under the ocean in a bathysphere.

1977
Marie Tharp and Bruce Heezen created a scientific map of the ocean floor.

1979
Sylvia Earle made the deepest <u>untethered</u> dive. She went down 1,250 feet in a diving suit.

19

BELIEVE IT OR NOT!

Humans have only explored a tiny amount of the ocean. The ocean is thought to be home to almost two million undiscovered <u>species</u>.

Phytoplankton are tiny living things that use sunlight for food. Phytoplankton only live in the sunlight zone.

Animals called narwhals are known as the unicorns of the sea. They have long horn-like tusks. Their tusks are actually long teeth.

When immortal jellyfish get old, they can turn themselves back into their young form! *Immortal* means that something can live forever.

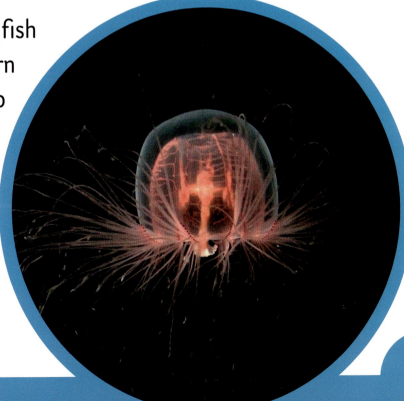

ARE YOU A GENIUS KID?

Now that you know so much about oceans, you can share your facts with other people! Before you go, let's test your knowledge to see whether you really are a genius kid.

Check back through the book if you are not sure.

1. What is the top layer of the ocean called?
2. Where is the deepest known part of the ocean?
3. Which zone is only in some deep trenches?

Answers: 1. The sunlight zone, 2. In the Mariana Trench, 3. The hadal zone

GLOSSARY

expedition — a journey made by a group of people with a particular purpose, such as exploration

habitats — the natural homes in which animals, plants, and other living things live

migrate — when animals move from one place to another

minerals — natural substances that are often hard

species — a group of very similar animals or plants that can create young together

surface — the top layer of a body of water

untethered — not using a cord or line to connect to something else

volcanoes — mountains that sometimes erupt, giving off very hot melted rock and gases

INDEX

animals 9–11, 13, 16, 21
coral polyps 9
fish 13
jellyfish 11, 21
maps 19

mountains 14
plants 10, 16
sunlight 8–10, 20
trenches 14, 16–17, 23
volcanoes 14